THE CHILD'S BOOK
ON THE FALL OF MAN

THE CHILD'S BOOK

of Bible Stories

with Practical Illustrations

ON THE FALL OF MAN

Thomas H. Gallaudet

Solid Ground Christian Books
Birmingham, Alabama USA

Solid Ground Christian Books
2090 Columbiana Rd, Suite 2000
Birmingham, AL 35216
205-443-0311
sgcb@charter.net
http://solid-ground-books.com

The Child's Book on the Fall of Man
WITH PRACTICAL ILLUSTRATIONS AND REMARKS

Thomas Hopkins Gallaudet (1787-1851)

Taken from 1834 edition by American Tract Society, New York

Solid Ground Classic Reprints

First printing of new edition June 2005

Cover work by Borgo Design, Tuscaloosa, AL
Contact them at nelbrown@comcast.net

ISBN: 1-932474-76-5

A Tribute to Thomas H. Gallaudet

Imagine the world without being able to read and to write. What would my life be like? Not to be able to read the Bible is the worst nightmare for me as a Deaf person. How will other deaf people "hear" the gospel without someone being able to read or write and to be able to communicate to them in American Sign Language?

I wanted to write a commendation to my hero, Rev. T.H. Gallaudet, who attended Yale College and was a congregational pastor. Early in 1817, Gallaudet met a deaf girl named, Alice Cogswell for the first time. He got her on his lap and showed her a hat; then he wrote h-a-t on the ground as Alice watched. She wrote h-a-t with Gallaudet's walking stick. That day and his experience with Alice was the most important in his life.

Alice's father, who was a doctor, met Gallaudet and he was crying because he wanted his daughter to get an education.

Gallaudet decided to look for a method of teaching the deaf students so he went on a trip to England and was not welcome by the "oral" school but instead, he found his way to France where there was a first school for the Deaf. The headmaster there introduced Gallaudet to the deaf teacher, Laurent Clerc and then, the school gave and sent America's first teacher, Laurent Clerc. While on a ship, Gallaudet and Clerc became close friends. Both taught each other English and French Sign Language.

As they arrived home, they established America's first school for the Deaf and now educated Alice Cogswell and many other children who were deaf and hard of hearing. There were more deaf schools established throughout America. In Kentucky, where I graduated from the school for the Deaf (in Danville), a man named John Jacob rode a horse all the way from Kentucky to

Connecticut to be trained under Laurent Clerc, so he could educate the Deaf children back in his home. This has changed the way we live today. I am thankful for the outcome. Today, all deaf people can read and write and now I can read the Bible and develop my personal relationship and get to know Jesus Christ better through reading. Now I am a pastor to a deaf congregation and we share the same language, American Sign Language, as well as the same culture. We are a close-knit group and I am blessed to enjoy my life much the same as everybody else today.

I commend you to buy the books Gallaudet wrote for children. He had a passion for children that Christ would be known by them.

> Pastor Jeremiah Ziehr
> Green River Area Deaf Fellowship
> Owensboro, Kentucky

TABLE OF CONTENTS

Personal Testimony from Deaf Pastor	v
An Address to the Child	3
Story One — The Permission	11
Story Two — The Prohibition	19
Story Three —The Penalty	27
Story Four — The Tempter	35
Story Five — The Temptation	43
Story Six — The Fall	53
Story Seven —The Remorse	61
Story Eight — The Excuses	69
Story Nine — The Curse	77
Story Ten — The Sentence	85

An Address to the Child who may read this Book

A little boy, who lived in a large city, once wandered far from home and could not find his way back. He had disobeyed his father in doing so, who told him not to go from the door of the house. At first, he was so much pleased with the new things which he saw, that he hardly thought how far he was going, or what he should tell his father on his return. But, by and by, he grew tired, and sat down on a step of a house to rest. He looked round him and saw that he was in a strange place. He had never been there before. All the houses were new to him, and the street looked very different from the one in which he lived. It was a long street; and, as he cast his eye down it, and remembered too that he had gone through many other streets, and turned many corners, before he got into it, he began to think that his father's house must be at a great distance, and that he could never find his way back to it.

He thought, too, how wicked he was in disobeying his father, and that it was this which had brought him into such trouble. This made him feel the more unhappy. He would have given all the pretty play-things he owned, if he could but be at home again, just as he was, a cheerful and happy child on the step before his father's house.

The evening was coming on, and the poor boy, as it grew dark, began to be greatly alarmed. He had been trying, for some time, by looking attentively at every one who passed him, to see if he could not discover an acquaintance, or, at least, somebody whom he knew by name, and to whom he might make himself known.

An Address to the Child who Reads

But none but strangers passed by, and no one took any particular notice of him. Why should they? They did not know that he was lost; for he had as yet sat on the step, sad and silent, without saying a word.

It grew darker, and he could scarcely see the faces of those who were going by him. He thought that he might perhaps have to spend the night in the street, and the tears began to roll down his cheeks. He sobbed, and at last cried aloud.

Many persons passing by must have heard him cry, but they did not stop to inquire what was the matter. Some were thinking so much about themselves and their own business, that they had no time to stop and be kind to a poor little crying boy. Others thought people should take care of their own children, and if they would not do it the children must suffer;—while some supposed that he belonged to the house on the step of which he was sitting, or at least in the neighborhood, and that his friends would soon come and take care of him.

The Child's Book on The Fall of Man

Poor boy! he might have sat there crying a long time, if a kind man who was passing by, and who loved little children, had not stopped and inquired the cause of his distress.

The boy told him all about it, and did not hide his disobedience to his father. He really felt sorry for having been guilty of this disobedience. He said that he did, and the man pitied him so much, and was so much pleased to see him sorry for his fault, that he told the boy, after asking his name and that of his father, that he would go with him and lead him safely home.

What a kind friend, and how happy the little wanderer was, as he entered once more the door of his father's house, to get back again to the arms of his dear parents.

How would you have felt, my dear child, had you been in his situation?—Would you have felt very thankful to the kind person who took so much pains to lead you home? — Would you have been truly sorry for your disobedience, and confessed it to your father, and asked his forgiveness, and resolved

An Address to the Child who Reads

never to do so again? —Would you have been very happy indeed to find yourself safe at home, once more under the care of a kind father and mother?

Have you ever thought that you have wandered a great way from your father,—from your Heavenly Father,—from God who made you, and who has done so much for you, and who has been kinder to you than any earthly parent can be?

Every time that you have done wrong, you have disobeyed God, and have been like the lost little boy, wandering from him. Perhaps you have never felt your danger in thus wandering from God. Wicked persons, in wandering from God, are going farther and farther from Heaven, that beautiful and happy place where those who get there are happier a great deal than the happiest little boys and girls are in their father's house here on earth.

Are you wandering from that delightful home, above the blue sky, where all are perfectly good and happy, and where your

The Child's Book on The Fall of Man

Heavenly Father wishes you to go after you die?—Are you wandering farther and farther from this Heavenly Father, who is inviting you to return to him, and has sent his Son to show you the way back, if you will but let him lead you?

Yes, Jesus Christ is like the kind man who led the lost little boy back to his home. He will take you kindly by the hand, and lead you back to God. Will you feel that you need such a kind friend? Will you put yourself under his care?—Will you be led by him to your Heavenly Father? Will you thus go to God, confessing your sins, beseeching him to forgive you for Christ's sake, and praying for the Holy Spirit to aid you in doing all this?

It is to show you how important it is for you to feel so, and to do so, that God has given you the Bible. You like to read other books, especially if they contain entertaining stories. —You were interested, were you not, in the story which I just told you about the little boy? Were you also interested while I tried to explain the use of that story, and to have it

An Address to the Child who Reads

lead you to think of God, and what you must do to have him for your everlasting friend?—Will you be interested in this book, if all the stories which are in it are taken from the Bible? And while I tell you these true stories from the Bible, and explain them in such a way as to do you good, and lead you to love God, and trust in Christ, and be prepared to go to your Heavenly Father's house in Heaven, when you die,—will you listen to me?—I hope you will, and that God will help me so to write, and you so to read, that this little book may lead you to love the Bible more than you have ever done before?

Remember, that the more you read and understand the Bible, the wiser you will be, and the more you love and obey it, the better and happier you will be. Pray daily to God for his Holy Spirit that you may thus read, understand, love, and obey that best of books, which He has given you to show you the way to Heaven.

Story One

THE PERMISSION

Story One

THE PERMISSION

When your father or mother tells you that you may go and play, they *permit* you to do it. Sometimes you ask them if you may look at a beautiful book full of pictures, and they say, "yes," and let you take it. They *permit* you to look at it. Or, what means the same thing, they give you *permission* to look at it. If your father has a garden, and he tells you that you may go into it and pick some fruit to eat, he gives you *permission* to do so.

What other things do your parents or teachers ever give you permission to do? See if you can think of some of them.

The Child's Book on The Fall of Man

Now I am ready to tell you the story about *the permission* which God gave Adam and Eve, to eat of the fruit which grew in the beautiful garden in which he placed them.

Adam and Eve, you know, were the first man and woman, and the beautiful garden in which they lived, was called Eden.

God made that garden for them to live in. It was a very delightful place. The air was pure and sweet.

The weather was neither too warm nor too cold. It was like one of our most pleasant days in the beginning of summer.

The garden was full of all kinds of beautiful trees, many of which bore the most delicious fruit; and a clear stream ran among them to water the garden, and to make the trees and plants grow.

It was there that Adam and Eve lived;— both good and happy; loving God and each other, and taking care of the garden.

God gave them *permission* to eat of the fruit that grew on all the trees, with the exception of one that stood in the middle of the garden. Of the fruit of *that* tree he

Story One – The Permission

commanded them not to eat. He told them that if they did eat of it, they should certainly die. I will tell you something more about this tree in the next story. What I wish you to think of now is, how very kind God was, in making that beautiful garden for Adam and Eve to live in, and in *permitting* them to eat of so many sorts of the most delicious fruit which grew on the trees of which the garden was full.

If some person who owned a very large and delightful garden, should tell you, that you might go into it at any time, and pick the fruit in it just when you chose, and as much as you chose, only taking care not to meddle with *a certain tree,* which he wished not to be touched,—you would think he was very kind indeed in giving you this permission.

You might wonder, perhaps, why he would not let you take some fruit from that tree, and he might not choose to tell you the reason for his doing so. Still, if he was a good man, you would know that he had some sufficient reason for doing it; and surely you would have no right to complain, for the fruit all belonged to him, and it was a great kindness in him to permit you to take any of it.

Suppose this person were your own father, and that he should let you go into his garden and eat of the different kinds of fruit, to show you what a *kind* father he was, and how much you ought to love him for all his kindness towards you. And suppose he should forbid you to take the fruit from one tree, to make you feel that he had a right to command you to do *as he pleased,* and to see whether you would feel so, and be obedient to him.

Ought you not to be very thankful to him for his kindness, and to love him for it and for all his goodness to you? Ought you not to feel that, while all the trees and the fruit in the garden belonged to him, he had a right, if he thought best, to forbid you to eat of the fruit of one of the trees?

Ought not Adam and Eve to have felt so towards God, their Heavenly Father, who

Story One – The Permission

created them, and did so much to make them good and happy?

"Yes," you say, "they certainly ought."

Well, take care then that *you* feel so towards your parents, and towards those who have the care of you. Be thankful when you are *permitted* to have, or to do, any thing which will make you good and happy. Do not complain when you are *forbidden* to take, or to do, any thing. Be contented. Be submissive. Be obedient. If you have not always been so, how much reason there is that you should be sorry for all your misconduct, and that you should pray to God to help you to feel right and to do right, in the future.

Story Two

THE PROHIBITION

Story Two

THE PROHIBITION

"The Prohibition," you say,—"that is a word which I do not understand."

But you know very well *the thing* which it means. Sometimes your father may have told you not to go near his table and meddle with the books and papers upon it. He gave you permission to play in the further corner of the room, but he *prohibited* you from coming near the table. When he rose from the table and went out of the room, he told you to remember his *prohibition*.

A mother told her daughter that she might go and walk in the garden, and look at the pretty flowers, and gather some of them from all the beds *excepting one,* to put together into a beautiful bouquet. The little girl was an obedient child, and did not forget the prohibition. She did not touch a single flower in the bed of tulips, for that was the one from which her mother had forbidden her taking the flowers.

Can you think of some things that *you* have been prohibited from taking or doing? Try and see if you can recall.

You will understand me when I tell you, that God *prohibited* Adam and Eve from eating the fruit of one tree in the middle of the garden in which they lived.

It was a prohibition that they could easily understand. There stood the tree in plain sight. God pointed it out to them, so that they could not be in any mistake with regard to it.

It was a prohibition which they could easily remember. Every time that they passed by the tree, they could not even look at it without thinking that it was *the only*

Story Two – The Prohibition

tree in the whole garden, of which they were forbidden to eat.

It was a prohibition which they knew God had a perfect right to make. The garden and all that grew in it was his. He made the trees and the delicious fruit which was on them. He caused the sun to shine and the gentle showers to fall upon them and make them grow. He could do as he chose with his own.

It was a prohibition of which Adam and Eve ought not in the least to complain. They had enough without using the fruit of that one tree. God had kindly given them a great abundance of the sweetest and best fruit with which the other trees were loaded. He had shown how much he loved them,—by creating them,—by giving them such curious and useful bodies, and souls that would live for ever and increase in goodness and in happiness, if they continued to love and obey him. He had placed them in a most delightful home, and

THE CHILD'S BOOK ON THE FALL OF MAN

was taking care of them like a tender and kind father.

It was a prohibition for which they must have known there was a good reason. God might wish in this way to let them show how willing and ready they were to obey his commands,—how cheerfully they could keep from what he prohibited and not even touch it. If he had given them no such prohibition, how could they have so well shown their obedience?

Is it not one of the best ways for you to show that you love your father, to keep from doing something which he has forbidden?

God might have wished, too, to see whether they were indeed his obedient children,—to *try them,* and let the angels and other beings see what Adam and Eve would do when thus tried.

That so good and kind a being as God had *some good reason* for giving them the prohibition, they could have no doubt. It

Story Two – The Prohibition

was a prohibition which it was not difficult for them to obey. It was not a hard thing *to be done.* It was just something *not to be done,* not to take the fruit from one tree.

How do you suppose you would have felt if you had been in that beautiful garden, and, like Adam and Eve, been forbidden to eat of the fruit of the tree in the midst of the garden?

You think, perhaps, that you would not have complained at all of the prohibition, but have been perfectly contented, and thankful to God for all his goodness.

But have you never felt uneasy and discontented when your parents or teachers have forbidden you to do, or to take something?—Have you never thought their prohibition too hard, and wished that you could be free from it?—Think a little, and you may find reason to believe, that if you had been under the same prohibition as Adam and Eve were, you would have thought it too strict, and wished that God had not made it.

THE CHILD'S BOOK ON THE FALL OF MAN

We shall see, in a few stories more, how they felt and acted. And let us try to see, too, whether *you* feel and act any better than they did.

Story Three

THE PENALTY

Story Three

THE PENALTY

A father who had a library in which there was a large and costly book of beautiful pictures, told his son that he must not take it down from its place. He said that he would show it to his son whenever it was best for him to see it, but that he must never take it down, and that if he did, he should shut him up in a room, and keep him there six hours.

The being shut up in the room six hours, was *the penalty* which the boy would have to suffer if he disobeyed his father.

If a man steals, the law says he must be put into prison. Imprisonment is *the penalty* for stealing.

The Child's Book on The Fall of Man

If a man kills another in anger, intending to do it, it is murder, and the law says he must be hung. To be hung is *the penalty* for murder.

Have *you* ever suffered any penalty for having broken the commands, or rules, of your parents or teachers?

When God forbade Adam and Eve to eat the fruit of the tree which was in the middle of the garden, he told them that if they disobeyed him, *they should surely die.—To* die was *the penalty* which they would have to suffer, if they should eat any of the fruit of that tree.

This meant a great deal more than that their bodies only should die. What more did it mean? Let me see if I can explain it to you?

When the body dies, it moves and acts no more. The eye cannot see any pleasant sights, nor the ear hear any pleasant sounds, nor the tongue taste any pleasant food. Death puts an end to all the pleasures of the body. It destroys them entirely.

Story Three – The Penalty

Now there is another kind of death spoken of in the Bible, which puts an end to, and destroys all the happiness of the soul.

When God told Adam and Eve that, if they disobeyed him, they should surely die, he meant that they should not only suffer the death of the body, but also the loss of his friendship and love, and of the happiness which they were enjoying in Eden. He meant that they should meet with a great deal of suffering in *this world* on account of their sin, and be exposed to endless suffering in the *world to come,* after their bodies should die.

This would be death indeed,—the death, or destruction of all their pure and holy pleasures, which made them so happy while they continued to love and obey God; the bringing upon them trouble and sorrow; the pains, sickness, and death of the body; and what was worse than all, the misery of being sent away from God and all good beings, to dwell for ever in a horrible place of punish-

The Child's Book on The Fall of Man

ment, with other sinful and unhappy beings like themselves.

Thus you see how the soul may *he* said to die as well as the body, by having all its happiness destroyed, and by dying and dying, as it were, for ever, in the endless sufferings that sin will bring upon it.

We should think that the penalty must have alarmed Adam and Eve very much, even if they did not fully understand the whole of it. They knew enough to make them fear greatly to disobey God. They knew that if they disobeyed him they would lose all the happiness which they were enjoying. They would no longer have God as their friend. He would both in this and the future world punish them severely. And they could see no way of escaping from this punishment. We should think that all this would have made them very careful, indeed, not to touch the forbidden tree, and not even *to wish* to touch it.

Do you not think it would have made you very much afraid to do so, if you had been in

Story Three – The Penalty

Eden, and if God had given you the same command which he gave Adam and Eve?

Why then are you not afraid *now* to sin against God? Do you know the awful penalty which he has threatened against sinners who do not feel truly sorry for their sins, and trust in Jesus Christ, and look to God for his Holy Spirit to help them to love and obey him? It is to be a miserable sinner for ever; to have *the soul be dying for ever; no* life in it; no right and good feelings, but all wicked and hateful ones; no kindness to others; no peace, no comfort, no happiness. It is to have *the soul dying for ever* in that miserable place where the wicked angels are, and where wicked men and women, and boys and girls, will go who do not repent of their sins and trust in the Savior. It is to have *the soul dying for ever,* having lost the friendship and favor of God, and cast out from heaven, with no hope of ever being permitted to go there.

My dear child, will you not fear this awful penalty?—Will you not go to God, and tell him how sorry you are that you have sinned against him? Will you not pray to him to give you his Holy Spirit to help you truly to repent of all your sins, to trust in the Lord Jesus Christ, to love and obey God, and to do all the good you can to others.—Go, go in this way, to your kind heavenly Father, and to the compassionate Savior, who are waiting to receive you, and, though your body must die, *your soul shall never die.*

Story Four

THE TEMPTER

Story Four

THE TEMPTER

William one day was standing at his father's door, who told him not to go away, as he wished him soon to go on an errand. A boy who used sometimes to play with William was passing by with a kite in his hand. "Come, William," said he, "come go with me, and help me fly my kite. There is a fine wind this morning, and I have got twine enough to let her go almost out of sight."

"I can't go," said William; "my father told me to stay here till he came back, when I am going on an errand for him."

"How soon will he be here?" said the boy. "I don't know," said William, "he may be half an hour."

"O! we shall have time enough then to go and fly the kite, and come back again."

"But I must not disobey my father; the Bible tells me that I should obey my parents in all things."

"If your father were here, I am sure he would let you go. Besides, you will be back before he comes, and he will not know any thing about it."

"But God will know all about it," said William; "he sees us at all times; he sees us now, and I dare not displease him by disobeying my father. *I shall not* go with you."

William did right. How much happier all little boys and girls would be, if they would do so too, whenever any one *tempts* them to do wrong, as the boy who had the kite tempted William to disobey his father.

When any one tries to lead you to do wrong, by telling you how happy you will be

Story Four – The Tempter

in doing it, or that you will get some good by doing it, that person, who thus tempts you is called *a tempter*. I dare say you have been tempted in this way. Think if you have not, and whether you have done as William did, or not. He was a good boy, and would not yield to the tempter who tried to lead him to do wrong.

There was a very wicked being who tempted Eve to do wrong in Eden. It was Satan, or the devil. He had once been a good angel, happy in loving and serving God. But he began to have wicked thoughts and feelings about God. He loved God no longer. He would not submit to God's government. There were other angels who felt and did as Satan did.

God could not let them remain in Heaven. Heaven, you know, is a holy and happy place. It would destroy the happiness of all the good beings who are there to have wicked ones among them. Besides, God means to have all the beings whom he has made, know that he has a *right* to govern them,—that it is *best* that he should govern them;—and that he *will* govern them. If they will not yield to his government, he must punish them for their disobedience.

How unhappy two or three disobedient and wicked children in a family, or even one such child, will make the whole family. The parents must govern and be obeyed, or all will be confusion and wretchedness.

God cast Satan and the wicked angels out of Heaven. He cast them down into hell, and there the Bible tells us they are kept "in everlasting chains, under darkness, unto the judgment of the great day."[1]

Satan found his way to Eden out of his dark and horrible prison. How he got out, or how he went to Eden, we do not know. We cannot even think how he did it. But we are sure of one thing, that God permitted him to do it, or else he never could have escaped from his prison. We are sure, too, that God had wise and good reasons for permitting Satan to do so; for God never does any thing

---

[1] Jude 6; cf. 2 Peter 2:4.

Story Four – The Tempter

without a reason, and all that he does is, like himself, holy, just and good.

Satan arrived in Eden. He had come to see if he could not tempt Adam and Eve to be wicked like himself, and disobey God. How much he must have hated God to wish to do this! How full of envy and of every bad feeling his heart must have been to wish to make Adam and Eve sinful and wretched like himself,—to have them cast out from the beautiful and pleasant garden in which they lived, and to lose the friendship of God!

Satan was *a tempter*. He was the first tempter of whom we have any account. What do you think of him? Do you wish to be like him?—"No, no," you say, "I hope I shall never be such a wicked and hateful being as he is."

Take care, then, lest you follow his example. Do you never have any wrong thoughts or feelings towards your parents or teachers? Do you never feel unwilling to submit to their government? If you think and feel so, you are disobeying God; for he commands you to obey your parents and teachers. You are fighting against *his government* as Satan did.

Do you never tempt any body to do wrong,—to do what you know, at the time, they ought not to do?—Think a little before you answer the question.

If you do, then you are *a tempter,* such as Satan was. Fear, fear, lest you may become *more* like him. Pray to God earnestly that he would keep you from following so dreadful an example.

Story Five

THE TEMPTATION

Story Five

THE TEMPTATION

Satan did not think it best to appear to Adam and Eve as he really was, a wicked and horrible being,—an angel of darkness just come from his dreadful prison-house. He became like a serpent, such as Adam and Eve had often seen, and of which they had no fear.

He found Eve alone, and near the forbidden tree. Adam was at a distance in some other part of the garden, taking care, perhaps, of the trees and plants, or gathering some fruit for food.

The Child's Book on The Fall of Man

The serpent, or rather Satan in the form of the serpent, spoke to Eve. He asked her, if God had indeed said that they should not eat of every tree of the garden.

"Oh! yes," said she, "we may eat of the fruit of the trees of the garden. But of the fruit of the tree which is in the midst of the garden, God hath said, 'ye shall not eat of it, neither shall ye touch it, lest ye die.'"[2]

Eve remembered very well what God had told her; and she ought immediately to have fled, as fast as she could, from one who she must have seen was trying to lead her to think that God's command was too strict. The very way in which Satan spoke to her, shows that this was what he wished to do.

And this is the way, my dear child, in which you may be tempted to do evil. Either your own wicked heart, or some wicked person, will lead you to think, at first, that the command of your parent, or teacher, or of God himself, is too strict. When you find

---

[2] Genesis 3:2,3.

Story Five – The Temptation

yourself *beginning* to think so,—stop. Stop at once. Look up to God. Pray to him in your mind, to help you to get rid of such thoughts, and to flee away from such a wicked person.

That is the only way in which you can be safe, and escape from the temptation. If Eve had done so, she would have been safe. But she stood there, to listen to what the tempter might still have to say to her.

What do you think he did next? Just what a wicked person is always ready to do when he is tempting another to sin. He told *a downright lie*. He dared to contradict what God had said, and to charge God himself with having uttered a falsehood.

"Ye shall not surely die," said Satan, "For God doth know that in the day ye eat thereof, then your eyes shall be opened, and ye shall be as gods, knowing good and evil."[3] He wished to make Eve believe that there was not the least danger in eating the forbidden fruit, and that besides this, both

---

[3] Genesis 3:4,5.

she and Adam would gain a great good by eating it. In some way or other, it would enable them to know many new and curious things, just as a person who has been blind and has his sight restored, will open his eyes, and soon be able to see ten thousand beautiful and wonderful objects. He told her that they would know so much about both good and evil things, that they would be like God himself in knowledge.

In this way Satan tried to make Eve feel that God was too strict in his command, and that he ought to have permitted Adam and her to eat of all the fruit in the garden, without any exception. He tried to make her feel uneasy and discontented, and to think that by eating the forbidden fruit she would be a great deal more happy and wise than she then was.

This is just the way with all temptations to sin. How have you thought and felt, when *you* have been tempted? You have not been contented with what you had. It has seemed to you, either from what you have thought

Story Five – The Temptation

yourself, or from what some wicked person has told you, that there was something which if you could get, or do, you would be a great deal happier. But then your parent, or teacher, or God himself in the Bible, has forbidden you to get, or to do, *that very thing*. *You* begin to feel uneasy at this prohibition. You think it is too strict. You doubt whether it is exactly right. You think of the punishment which is threatened against you, if you disobey. You hope that in some way or other you will escape this punishment, or that there is some mistake about it, and that you are in no danger of suffering it at all. Your own wicked heart, or some wicked companion, tells you so, and the temptation begins to lead you to disobedience.

Now when you think and feel so again, remember Eve. Remember how Satan tempted her; how he lied and tried to deceive her. And will you let *a lie* deceive you, and lead you to disobey God, and have him displeased with you?

The Child's Book on The Fall of Man

Every temptation to sin, whether it comes from your own wicked heart, or from a wicked companion, is *a lie*. It is just such a lie as Satan told Eve. If you believe it; if you yield to it; if you do the wicked thing; it is like saying, as Satan did, that *God is a liar*. It is saying that you do not believe that what God says is true. He says that he will certainly punish sinners with a most awful punishment. When you yield to temptation and sin against him, do you not say, by your conduct, that you do not think that you shall really suffer such a punishment.

Dare, you thus, as Satan did, charge the great God with falsehood? Dare you say or think that you can sin against him, and escape from the punishment which he has threatened against the wicked?—What he threatens he will do. "It is a fearful thing to fall into the hands of the living God." "Fear him who after he hath killed, hath power to cast into hell: yea, I say unto you, fear him."[4]

---

[4] Hebrews 10:31; Luke 12:5.

Story Five – The Temptation

Fear to sin against him. Fear *the beginning of* wicked thoughts and feelings. Pray earnestly to God for his Holy Spirit that you may be immediately delivered from them.

Story Six

THE FALL

Story Six

THE FALL

Once when Jesus Christ was teaching the people, he wished to make them think how foolish it would be for a person to listen to the good things which he was teaching, and then go away and act directly contrary to them. He said it would be as foolish as for a man to build his house upon the sand, without putting any stones under it for a foundation for it to stand upon. In a great storm of wind and rain, and with the waters of a raging stream dashing against the house, it would fall, and *the fall* of it would be great.

The Child's Book on The Fall of Man

So we say, if a boy or girl, a man or woman, has for some time conducted themselves well, and all at once yields to temptation, and commits a great sin, that he or she has *fallen*. And in this story, I shall tell you of *the fall* of Adam and Eve. Eve, however, fell first, as we shall see.

After hearing what Satan had to say, Eve did not reprove him for saying it, which shows that she was doing wrong in thus listening to so wicked a tempter. She began soon to look more attentively at the forbidden fruit. Its appearance led her to suppose that, like the other fruit in the garden, it would be "good for food." Then it looked fair and ripe, and with its beautiful color was "pleasant to the eyes." She thought, too, of what Satan had just told her, and felt that the fruit was "to be desired to make one wise."

Poor, foolish, sinful Eve! How could she thus dare to believe what Satan told her, and doubt the truth of God's threatening!

She drew near the tree, and stretched out her hand, and took of the fruit and ate

Story Six – The Fall

it. And having sinned herself, just as all other wicked persons do, she soon tempted Adam to sin likewise.

It was not long before he came that way and saw what Eve had done. The Bible does not tell us how he felt or what he said; neither does it tell us what Eve said to him.

As Satan, however, tempted her, so she tempted Adam. She gave him some of the fruit, and he also ate of it.

They fell. They fell from the state in which they had been,—from being good and happy,—from being obedient to God and enjoying his friendship and love,—into sin;—into disobedience to God and the beginning to suffer that punishment which he had threatened, if they should break his command.

This was *the fall,* and it brought sickness, and pain, and sorrow, and death into the world. It brought sin, too, the worst of all evils. Adam and Eve's children were sinners. And *their* children were sinners,— and so on down till this time. All, all have

The Child's Book on The Fall of Man

sinned,—you and I, and every body.[5] We have sinned as Adam and Eve did. For do you not remember, my dear child, how often you have had thoughts and feelings, and said and done things, which you knew, at the time, to be wicked,—just as Eve knew it was wicked for her to wish to eat the forbidden fruit, and to take some from the tree and eat it.

You wonder, perhaps, when you read the story about them, that they could not be contented with all that delicious fruit with which the trees were loaded, but must listen to what a wicked and deceitful tempter said, and for the sake of eating of the fruit of one more tree, expose themselves to the terrible displeasure of God.

You wonder that, while God had done so much to make them good and happy, they could forget it all, and disbelieve what he said, and disobey one who had been so full of kindness to them.

Ah! my child, *all sin* is just the same kind of folly, and unbelief, and unthankfulness.

---

[5] Romans 3:10-18,23.

Story Six – The Fall

Has not God been very kind to *you?*—Has he not done a great deal to make you good and happy? Has he not given you all that you need, and all that is best for you? If you love and obey him, and those whom he has placed over you to take care of you, will you not have the highest kind of happiness which you can have in this world?

Why do you so often wish to reach after and get *some forbidden fruit;* something which you know your parents or teachers have prohibited, or which God himself has prohibited you from having or doing?

Ah! while you wonder at poor, sinful Adam and Eve, wonder at your own folly and wickedness! See, how exactly you are like them. Feel sorry for having committed the same kind of sin which they did. Do not feel proud and boastful, and say that if *you* had been in Eden, and been tempted by Satan as they were, you would not have acted as they did.

You *have acted* as *they* did. You are guilty as they were. You are exposed to that awful punishment with which God

The Child's Book on The Fall of Man

threatened *them,* if they should disobey him. You are exposed to it, and must endure it all, both in this and the future world, unless you go to God,—sorry, humble, broken-hearted on account of your sins,—beseeching him, because Christ died for sinners, to forgive you,—trusting in this Savior,—and praying that God would lead you, by his Holy Spirit, to be like Christ.

You have been *like Adam;* will you not wish, and strive, and pray to be *like Christ?*

Story Seven

THE REMORSE

Story Seven

THE REMORSE

Suppose a boy were alone in a room in the house in which he lived, and knew that in a trunk near the window there was some money belonging to his father. The wicked thought comes into his mind, that a key which he has in his pocket will unlock the trunk, and that he can take a dollar from it, without any one's knowing it. He thinks of all the pretty things that he can buy for a dollar, and how happy they will make him. He yields to the temptation. He takes the dollar, locks up the trunk, and goes down stairs and tries to look as if nothing had happened.

The Child's Book on The Fall of Man

He is kept at home all the day and cannot spend the dollar. When evening comes he goes to bed, as usual, in good season, and lest some one should find the dollar in his pocket, he hides it in a closet, where he thinks it will be safe till the morning.

Do you think he would pray to God that evening, before lying down to sleep?—No, he would not pray, as long as he meant to keep the dollar. But he would feel unhappy, and very unhappy indeed if it was the *first time* that he had stolen any thing.

There would be several things to make him feel unhappy. He would feel *ashamed of himself,* to think that be could be a thief, and steal money too from his own father, who had been so kind to him.

He would have pretty strong fears lest he should *be found out,* and have to suffer disgrace and punishment.

He would feel too that what he had done was *wrong*—that he had been guilty of

Story Seven – The Remorse

great wickedness,—that God knew it, and that he could not escape the displeasure of God. He would feel that he *deserved* this displeasure, and that sooner or later it might reach him.

These thoughts and feelings, as he lay his head down on his pillow, would trouble him so as to keep him awake, and make him very wretched indeed.

Such thoughts and feelings, after a person has done some wicked thing, and is thinking about it,—is called *remorse*.—I dare say you know what it is. For although you may never have stolen any thing, yet you have done things which at the time you knew to be wrong, and have been very unhappy afterwards while thinking about your conduct.

Sometimes this remorse has been so great in persons who have stolen, or even in those who have murdered some one, that they have confessed their guilt, when nobody suspected them, and have given themselves up to punishment.

The Child's Book on The Fall of Man

Nothing can cause as great suffering in this world as remorse; and it will be one of the principal causes of the sufferings of the wicked in the future world.

Adam and Eve felt this remorse most deeply after they had eaten the forbidden fruit. They felt their shame and guilt. They felt how ungrateful and disobedient they had been to their kind, Heavenly Father. They felt afraid to meet him. They dreaded his displeasure. They trembled at the thought of the punishment which he had threatened, and which they knew they deserved.—They lamented their folly in believing what Satan had told them. They found that they did indeed *know both good and evil,* but in a way far different from that which he had promised, and which they had expected.

Wretched in looking back upon what they had done, and in looking forward to what they must suffer,—they had nothing to make them happy; nothing in themselves; in the delightful garden that was around them; or in God, should he again come to meet them as he had done before.

Story Seven – The Remorse

He *did come* to meet them. It was in the cool of the day, and they heard his voice in the garden.

How glad they would have been to hear that voice if they had not sinned,—if the fruit on the forbidden tree had remained untouched. But they were alarmed by the voice. They dreaded to meet the great and glorious being from whom it came. Trembling and fleeing from it "they hid themselves from the presence of the Lord God amongst the trees of the garden."[6]

Have *you* not felt just so when you have done wrong, and were afraid of being found out? Sometimes you may have run away and hid yourself as Adam and Eve did; and at other times, you have wished to avoid the eye of some one,—of your parent or teacher, and would have hid yourself from their look if you could have done it.

How unpleasant such feelings are! But how happy a person feels when he can look every body full in the face,—fearing no eye

---

[6] Genesis 3:8.

The Child's Book on The Fall of Man

that shall examine him, and no tongue that shall ask him a question.

How happy you have felt when you could run and meet your father, or mother, or teacher, and hear their voice, and catch their kind look, and let them see that *you look* as an obedient and happy child always does.

Be obedient to them. Be obedient to God, if you wish to enjoy this happiness. Remember how Adam and Eve hid themselves in the garden, and pray to God that he would keep you from *sinning,* that so you may be kept from *shame and fear.*

Story Eight

THE EXCUSE

Story Eight

THE EXCUSE

How very hard it is when a person has done wrong, to feel sorry for it, and to confess it, and ask to be forgiven.

How often when *you* have done wrong, have you tried, on being told of it, to make some *excuse* for it? You forgot, you said, all about what your parent or teacher had commanded. You did not suppose that they meant exactly so. You did not intend to do just as you did. It was much worse than you thought it would be. You were mistaken

The Child's Book on The Fall of Man

about it. A companion told you there could be no harm in doing it. He led you on to do it. He did it more than half himself. You never would have thought of doing it, if he had not tempted you.

Just so Adam and Eve began to make excuses, when God called them out from their hiding place and they came and stood trembling before him.

"Hast thou eaten," said he to Adam, "of the tree, whereof I commanded thee that thou shouldst not eat?"[7]

"The woman whom thou gavest to be with me, she gave me of the tree, and I did eat."[8]—This was Adam's reply. How unwilling he was, frankly and humbly to confess his guilt. How ready he was, if possible, to make some excuse for it. How he tried to throw the blame on Eve, as if he could not avoid doing as she urged him to do, and could not refuse to accept the forbidden fruit from her hand.

---

[7] Genesis 3:11.
[8] Genesis 3:12.

Story Eight – The Excuses

God then inquired of Eve; "what is this that thou hast done?"[9]—She too was ready with an excuse. Her reply was; "the serpent beguiled me," or told me pleasant and deceitful things about the fruit, which led me without hardly thinking of what I did to pluck it,—"and I did eat."[10]

Oh! how much better it would have been for both Adam and Eve to have cast themselves at the feet of their Heavenly Father, and with a heart-felt sorrow for their sin to have confessed it, and besought him to forgive them!

Do you not think, also, that it would always have been better for you to have done the same, when you have done wrong? Think of this. Look back and see *how you felt* when you tried to make excuses for what you knew to be wicked, and deserving of blame or of punishment. And then think *how you felt* when, at any time, you confessed your guilt, and was sorry for it,

---

[9] Genesis 3:13a.
[10] Genesis 3:13b.

and asked forgiveness. Which way of acting do you now think was the best?

When you made excuses, your guilt seemed to be increasing; or at any rate your wrong and disobedient feelings grew worse. You felt, all the while, a still stronger unwillingness than ever, to yield to the authority of your parent or teacher. Your excuses, too, were so much like telling a falsehood, that you felt a good deal of the shame and self-reproach that a liar does. You usually have found that your excuses were not taken, and that it turned out worse for you in the end than if you had told the exact truth and confessed your guilt. You have found, too, that after making such excuses, you were the more likely to do similar things again and thus get into new troubles.

On the other hand, when you have honestly confessed your fault, and felt sorry, and asked forgiveness,—how relieved and happy you have been if this forgiveness was granted. And even if you have had to suffer punishment, how much lighter it has

Story Eight – The Excuses

seemed, and how differently your parent or teacher has regarded you, while you have been suffering it. And when it has all been over, and you have seen that your word could be believed, and that your parent or teacher loved you again, and wished to encourage and help you to behave well, how delightful this was to you, and how you hoped that in future you would be enabled to avoid the fault that you had committed.

Remember, too, that all this is equally true with regard to God.

If you try, as Adam and Eve did, to find out excuses for the sins which you have committed against God, your heart will grow harder in sin. You will begin to think less of the evil of sin. You will think less and less of the danger and guilt of sinning against God. You will keep on sinning,— wandering farther and farther from God,— and making the punishment for your sins greater and greater.

But if you confess your sins to God, and feel truly sorry for them, and trust in Jesus

The Child's Book on The Fall of Man

Christ, God has promised to forgive your sins. He has told us so in the Bible in these words which he directed the apostle John to write; "If we confess our sins, he is faithful and just, to forgive us our sins, and to, cleanse us from all unrighteousness."[11] We also read in Proverbs; "He that covereth his sins shall not prosper, but whoso confesseth and forsaketh them shall have mercy."[12]

Think what a blessing it is to have all your sins forgiven, and to be led by the Holy Spirit to avoid sinning in future,—to have God for your friend, and to become prepared when you die, to go and be with him and with Jesus Christ for ever.

---

[11] 1 John 1:9.
[12] Proverbs 28:13.

Story Nine

THE CURSE

Story Nine

THE CURSE

Sometimes wicked men are angry at others, and say that they wish that God would send them to hell. This is called *cursing*. I have heard boys *curse* and swear. It is sad to hear them, and to think what wicked hearts they must have, thus to take the name of God in vain, and break one of his commands, and be exposed to his dreadful displeasure. Can it be that the little boy or girl who is reading this book, ever uses bad words, or takes the name of God in vain? I hope not. If you ever have done so, think, think what a wicked thing it is.

The Child's Book on The Fall of Man

But there is another kind of cursing. It is when God says that some great evil must come upon some person, or place, or thing. Then it surely *will come,* for God is almighty, and can do whatever he pleases. What he says, is true, and will always come to pass.—Such a curse is dreadful indeed. You remember that Jesus Christ said, that when he comes to judge all mankind, he will say unto the wicked, on his left hand; "depart from me, *ye cursed,* into everlasting fire, prepared for the devil and his angels."[13]

The *first curse* which we read of in the Bible is that which God uttered against the serpent, or Satan, who tempted Eve. You can read it in the third chapter of Genesis.

There is one part of this curse to which I wish you particularly to attend,—for it is accompanied with *a great blessing* to you and to me, and to all mankind.

God said that *the seed of the woman should bruise the head of the serpent.*[14]

---

[13] Matthew 25:41.
[14] Genesis 3:15.

Story Nine – The Curse

By *the seed of the woman* is meant some one of the descendants of Eve. She was to have children, and these again would have children, and these again would have children, and so on. All these would be *the descendants* of Eve, or her seed. Now God declared that one of these descendants should bruise the head of the serpent.

Poisonous snakes, you know, are sometimes found in the fields and roads, and the men or boys who see them, often take a large stick or stone and beat them on the head till they are killed.

Now as Satan had taken the form of a serpent when he tempted Eve, *to bruise the head of that serpent* would mean, *to bruise the head of Satan,* that is, to weaken and destroy him, so that he could do no more harm. For you know Satan has done, and is still doing, a great deal of evil in the world. In some way which we cannot understand, God has permitted him to tempt many persons to sin, as he did Eve. You must remember, however, that this is no more an excuse for *their* sinning than it was for *hers*. God will give all who look to him for it in sincere prayer, and trusting in Christ,—strength to resist Satan and to overcome all his temptations.

From among the descendants of Eve *a person would arise who should weaken, and finally destroy, the power of Satan.*

And that person has come. It is *the Lord Jesus Christ, the Son of God. As* a man, he is one of the descendants of Eve. Mary, you know, was his mother. And if you go back to *her* father and mother, and to *their* father and mother, and so on, you will at last get back to Eve,—the mother, as she is called, of them all and of all mankind.

It was four thousand years before Christ was born when God pronounced the curse upon Satan in Eden, and declared that the seed of the woman should bruise his head. You see how wonderfully this has come to pass.

Satan has been trying, ever since he tempted Eve, to lead men to become the enemies of God; and those who listen to his

Story Nine – The Curse

temptations, and are wicked, like him, the Bible calls *his children*.

Jesus Christ came into the world to lead men to love God, and to become his friends and the friends of each other. Satan, therefore, hates and opposes Christ. But Christ is almighty. He has already *bruised the serpent's head*. While on earth, you remember how he overcame the temptations of Satan, and how he cast out devils, and gave his disciples power to cast them out.

He once said that he saw "Satan as lightning fall from heaven;"[15] probably meaning by this that the time had come for the great downfall of Satan's power to do evil.

The Bible tells us that it was thus to destroy the power of Satan that Christ came into the world; "For this purpose the Son of God was manifested, that he might destroy the works of the devil."[16] And when he died on the cross, then it was that Satan and all the wicked angels felt that they were indeed overcome. Then Christ was a complete conqueror over

---

[15] Luke 10:18.
[16] 1 John 3:8.

them. He may permit them, for wise reasons, to do some more evil in the world. But they can do nothing without his permission, and at last they will be shut up forever in their dismal prison-house, never again to leave it, or disturb the peace of God's government over his obedient creatures.

I have said thus much about Satan, my dear child, because be *may tempt you.* He may lead you to have wicked thoughts and desires; and I wish you to know *where* you must look for strength to overcome them. Look to Jesus Christ, *the seed of the woman, who was to bruise the serpent's head.* If you look to him for this strength, and trust in him,—he will give it to you, and "the God of peace shall bruise Satan under your feet."[17] Remember that Christ has completely conquered this great enemy of all good, and that he can enable *you* to conquer him also. *In the strength of Jesus Christ,* "Resist the devil, and he will flee from you."[18]

---

[17] Romans 16:20.
[18] James 4:7.

Story Ten

THE SENTENCE

Story Ten

THE SENTENCE

If a school-master should find out that one of the boys had been very angry with another, and struck him so hard as to hurt his eye badly, he would do right to call the two boys before him, in the presence of the whole school, and inquire into the matter.

After inquiring, he feels that it is his duty to punish the boy who struck the other. He makes him stand on a stool so that all the scholars can see him. He says to him; "for your very bad conduct in getting

The Child's Book on The Fall of Man

angry and striking your school-fellow, you must bring your dinner to school for three days, and stay here locked up from twelve to two o'clock, and your dinner must be nothing but bread and water."

This *telling* the boy what his punishment would be, was *the sentence* which the master passed upon him

A judge *sentences* a man who is found guilty of stealing, to imprisonment; and a man who is found guilty of murder, to death.

There was a sentence which God passed upon Adam and Eve, after he had pronounced the curse upon Satan. How sad and guilty they must have felt while receiving it!

He told Eve that she should have much pain and sorrow, and Adam that he should suffer greatly also. On account of his sin, the whole earth would be cursed. It would begin to bring forth thorns and thistles. A great change would take place. Things would look very different from what they had done in Eden. Adam and Eve would no longer eat the delicious fruit with which

Story Ten – The Sentence

that garden abounded. They were soon to leave it, never to return. Adam must labor and toil hard to raise his food from the ground by digging and cultivating it. And, at last, they must both die, and their bodies be mingled with the dust.

Sin was the cause of these evils to Adam and Eve; and look round, and see how much pain, and sorrow, and trouble sin still causes.

The sentence of death has passed upon all men, for that all have sinned. *You suffer because you are a sinner*. If you live, you will have, like Adam and Eve, to meet with pain, and sorrow and trouble. And, at last, you will die. God says to you, as he did to Adam; "dust thou art, and unto dust shalt thou return."[19]

Think of the evil of sin. It is a great evil because it is committed against God. Whenever you have sinned, *you have made this evil greater*. Ought you not to repent,—will you not repent of all your sins, and go to Christ, and love him, and obey his commands?

---

[19] Genesis 3:19.

The Child's Book on The Fall of Man

We are told that, after passing sentence upon Adam and Eve, God drove them out of Eden. This was a part of their punishment, and they must have felt it very severely. They knew that they never would be permitted to return, and enjoy again its pleasant walks and shades, and breathe its pure and fragrant air, and eat its delicious fruits. Here they had felt safe under the protection of their Almighty friend. He had visited them and conversed with them; (at least, we have reason to think so.) They had been happy in loving and obeying him, and in loving and doing good to each other. All their wants had been satisfied, and if they had only been contented and obedient, this delightful garden, with all its pure and holy pleasures, would still have been their home. What a painful thought to think that they were now to lose this home, and to go forth to endure pain, and toil, and sorrow, and death, in a world cursed and changed on account of their sin!

Story Ten – The Sentence

Unhappy Adam and Eve! Think how they must have felt as they took their last look of Eden!

But there is a brighter and more beautiful, a happier and lovelier place than Eden was. It is Heaven, the Paradise of God. There is no sin there, and no temptation to sin;—no pain, or sickness;—no trouble or sorrow. All is holiness and peace. All is perfect happiness. There is no fear of a change. The joys of Heaven will be eternal.[20]

Its inhabitants will be improving constantly in knowledge, in goodness, and in happiness. Their delight will consist in learning more of God and of Jesus Christ; in loving and serving them; and in rejoicing to do good to all around them.

What were the delicious fruits, the fragrant air, and all the pleasures of the garden in which Adam and Eve lived, to the joys of the Heavenly Paradise.

How wretched were Adam and Eve in being cast out from Eden! How will *you*

---

[20] Psalm 16:11; Matthew 25:46.

The Child's Book on The Fall of Man

feel, my dear child, should *you* be so unhappy as to be shut out forever from the Eden above!

You need not be. There is a *sure way*, in which you can gain admittance there, never to be cast out. Jesus Christ is that way. He died on the cross that the way to Heaven might be opened for you. He is ready and waiting to take you by the hand, and lead you into this way. Will you go to him? You know, while on earth, he said, "Suffer little children to come unto me, and forbid them not."[21]

Will you go to this kind and compassionate Savior? He loved you so much,—yes, *you* who are reading this book, that he came down from Heaven and died on the cross, on purpose to save you! Will you any longer delay to go to him?

Go to Christ as a poor, sick, and almost dying man looks to the physician who comes to see him, and feels that his only hope of life is in what this kind and skillful physician will do for him.

---

[21] Luke 18:16.

Story Ten – The Sentence

Go to Christ, feeling as Peter did when he was sinking in the waters, and was near drowning, and felt that he had no strength in himself, and cried out "Lord, save me, or I perish."[22]

Go to Christ, feeling as the repenting publican did when he "smote upon his breast, saying, 'God be merciful to me a sinner.'"[23]

Go to Christ, feeling that *you are indeed a sinner,* and that the law of God justly sentences you to punishment, as it did Adam and Eve.

Go to Christ, feeling that lost in yourself, without any goodness and without any strength of your own, you come to be saved by him, and to receive this salvation as a free gift which you do not at all deserve.

Will you do this? Will you now go alone and try to do it? Will you pray to God for his Holy Spirit to aid you in doing it? He has

---

[22] Matthew 14:30.
[23] Luke 18:13.

said, "Ask, and ye shall receive; seek, and ye shall find; knock and it shall be opened onto you."–"Him that cometh to me I will in no wise cast out."[24]

THE END

---

[24] Matthew 7:7; John 6:37.

Other Gallaudet Titles

In addition to *The Child's Book on the Fall* we are delighted to announce our intention to publish several more of his titles.

The Child's Book on the Soul
Perhaps the most remarkable of all Gallaudet's works is this little double volume. He speaks in a way that a four or five year old can grasp his words, and learn of the infinite and eternal value of their soul.

The Child's Book on Repentance
Gallaudet uses a series of dialogues to lead the children to consider the nature of genuine, biblical repentance. Most illuminating.

The Child's Book on Natural Theology
Gallaudet uses a series of dialogues to lead the child (a little older than in *The Child's Book on the Soul*) to understand everything that can be learned about God from the world around us.

Scripture Biography for the Young
Gallaudet does a masterful job opening and applying lessons from all the leading characters from the Old Testament. I have read nothing like them!
> **Volume One:** *Adam to Joseph*
> **Volume Two:** *The Life of Moses*
> **Volume Three:** *Joshua, Judges, Ruth*
> **Volume Four:** *Samuel and David*

Other Solid Ground Titles

In addition to the book which you hold in your hand, Solid Ground is honored to offer many other uncovered treasure, many for the first time in more than a century:

THE CHILD AT HOME by John S.C. Abbott
MY BROTHER'S KEEPER: *Letters to a Younger Brother* by J.W. Alexander
THE KING'S HIGHWAY: *10 Commandments for the Young* by Richard Newton
THE LIFE OF JESUS CHRIST FOR THE YOUNG by Richard Newton
LET THE CANNON BLAZE AWAY by Joseph P. Thompson
THE STILL HOUR: *Communion with God in Prayer* by Austin Phelps
COLLECTED WORKS of James Henley Thornwell (4 vols.)
CALVINISM IN HISTORY *by Nathaniel S. McFetridge*
OPENING SCRIPTURE: *Hermeneutical Manual by Patrick Fairbairn*
THE ASSURANCE OF FAITH *by Louis Berkhof*
THE PASTOR IN THE SICK ROOM *by John D. Wells*
THE BUNYAN OF BROOKLYN: *Life & Sermons of I.S. Spencer*
THE NATIONAL PREACHER: Sermons from 2nd Great Awakening
FIRST THINGS: First Lessons God Taught Mankind *Gardiner Spring*
BIBLICAL & THEOLOGICAL STUDIES *by 1912 Faculty of Princeton*
THE POWER OF GOD UNTO SALVATION *by B.B. Warfield*
THE LORD OF GLORY *by B.B. Warfield*
A GENTLEMAN & A SCHOLAR: *Memoir of J.P. Boyce* by J. Broadus
SERMONS TO THE NATURAL MAN *by W.G.T. Shedd*
SERMONS TO THE SPIRITUAL MAN *by W.G.T. Shedd*
HOMILETICS AND PASTORAL THEOLOGY *by W.G.T. Shedd*
A PASTOR'S SKETCHES 1 & 2 *by Ichabod S. Spencer*
THE PREACHER AND HIS MODELS *by James Stalker*
A HISTORY OF PREACHING *by Edwin C. Dargan*
LECTURES ON THE HISTORY OF PREACHING *by J. A. Broadus*
THE SCOTTISH PULPIT *by William Taylor*
THE SHORTER CATECHISM ILLUSTRATED *by John Whitecross*
THE CHURCH MEMBER'S GUIDE *by John Angell James*
THE SUNDAY SCHOOL TEACHER'S GUIDE *by John A. James*
CHRIST IN SONG: *Hymns of Immanuel from All Ages* by Philip Schaff
COME YE APART: *Daily Words from the Four Gospels* by J.R. Miller
DEVOTIONAL LIFE OF THE S.S. TEACHER *by J.R. Miller*

Call us Toll Free at 1-877-666-9469
Send us an e-mail at sgcb@charter.net
Visit us on line at solid-ground-books.com

Printed in the United States
77275LV00001B/298-396